EVONNE GOOLAGONG
SMASHER FROM AUSTRALIA

EVONNE GOOLAGONG
SMASHER FROM AUSTRALIA

by Julian May

Published by Crestwood House, Inc., Mankato, Minnesota 56001. Published simultaneously in Canada by J. M. Dent and Sons, Ltd. Library of Congress Catalog Card Number: 74-31951. International Standard Book Number: 0-913940-19-4. Text copyright © 1975 by Julian May Dikty. Illustrations copyright © 1975 by Crestwood House, Inc. All rights reserved. No part of this book may be reproduced in any form without written permission from the publisher, except for brief passages included in a review. Printed in the United States of America.

Designed by William Dichtl

Crestwood House, Inc., Mankato, Minn. 56001

PHOTOGRAPHIC CREDITS:

Australian Information Service: 2, 16, 31, 33, 35, 47. John Fairfax & Sons, Ltd. © photos courtesy Leo Armati, Sydney Morning Herald: 8, 9, 10, 11, 12, 13, 46. UPI: cover, 6, 14, 17, 19, 21, 22, 23, 24, 26, 27, 30, 32, 36, 37, 38, 39, 40, 41, 44, 45. Wide World: 20, 28, 29, 42, 43, 48. World Team Tennis: 34.

EVONNE GOOLAGONG
SMASHER FROM AUSTRALIA

Australia is an old, old land. The rocks are very ancient. So are the plants and animals. And when explorers first came to Australia, they found Stone Age people living there.

These people were called Aboriginals. They had dark skins and wavy hair that was black or blond. Some scientists said that Aboriginals were the oldest kind of human still on earth.

White settlers came to Australia and took over the land. But the Aboriginals did not die out. Many hid in the desert and lived as they always had. Others gathered near the growing towns and worked for the whites.

The two races mixed. People who were part Aboriginal lived very much like white Australians. They forgot the ancient ways of the tribes.

One such family was the Goolagongs. Their name meant either "trees by still waters" or "nose of the kangaroo." Ken Goolagong, the father, was a sheep-shearer. He and his wife, Linda, lived in Barellan. It was a small town about 300 miles from Sydney, Australia's largest city. Sheep, wheat, and fruit were raised there.

Ken and Linda Goolagong didn't have a lot of money. But they never felt too poor, either.

Evonne was the third Goolagong child. She was so shy that she would hide when a stranger came to the house.

Evonne's brother Ian and sister Janelle play on the simple backyard tennis court of the Goolagong home at Barellan, New South Wales, Australia.

Australian people love tennis. Even a tiny place like Barellan had tennis courts. And the Goolagong children spent a lot of time there. When Evonne was four, she chased balls for her older brother and sister.

When she was five, she decided she wanted to play. Somebody lent her a racquet. The little girl learned the game very quickly. She was graceful and fast on her feet. And for such a little girl, she was very strong.

Evonne Goolagong was a natural athlete. When she played tennis, she forgot to be shy.

Evonne and part of her family get together before a match in Sydney. In the back row are her sister-in-law, Lauris, her sister Janelle, and Mrs. Linda Goolagong, her mother. In the center are her brother Ian, her sister Gail, and Mr. Ken Goolagong, her father. Her little brother Martin holds Evonne's racquet.

When she was nine, an aunt gave her a racquet all her own. She slept with it! She had now become such a good player that adults noticed her. A farmer named Bill Kurtzmann was president of the local tennis club. He took Evonne to her first tournament when she was ten.

It was in the town of Narrandera. When Evonne and Mr. Kurtzmann got there, they found out that the tournament was for adults.

Little Evonne played in the women's singles anyway. And she won.

9

When Evonne was 12, she spent summer vacations at Sydney with the Vic Edwards family, learning all she could about the game of tennis.

A traveling tennis clinic came to Barellan. The pro, Colin Swan, saw Evonne play. He was so amazed that he called his boss in Sydney.

"There's this Aboriginal kid," he said, "who just flows around the court! She's a natural. She could be a champion."

Swan's boss was Vic Edwards, a famous tennis teacher. He came out to watch Evonne. When they met, the little girl was so shy that she could hardly speak. In months to come, Mr. Edwards became Evonne's friend. During the summer holidays, she visited with the Edwards family in Sydney. She took lessons and entered some tournaments.

And she began to win.

Young Evonne talks to Australian champion Roy Emerson before a match in Sydney. Emerson won the men's singles title at Wimbledon in 1964 and 1965. He won the Forest Hills championship in 1961 and 1964.

When Evonne was 13, Vic Edwards said: "She can be a world-beater. By 1974, I predict she will be a great champion."

Not too many people took him seriously. But many hoped he was right. Evonne was a charming little girl. Very few Aboriginals had a chance to do great things in Australia—much less in the whole world. If Evonne became famous, it might help other Aboriginals, too.

Evonne herself didn't think much about her race. She had never faced prejudice as other Aboriginals had. She was just a little girl who loved to play tennis.

Vic Edwards, Evonne's coach and foster father, has guided her throughout her tennis career.

In 1965, when Evonne was 14, she won a major tennis title. It was the New South Wales under-15 championship.

Mr. Edwards came to see Mr. and Mrs. Goolagong. He said: "Now Evonne needs special tennis coaching. She should study tennis all year, not just during summer holidays, or she will not become great."

Edwards told the Goolagongs that he wanted to adopt Evonne as his daughter.

"She will live with me and my wife Eva," he said. "We have five daughters. Evonne will go to school with our daughter, Patricia. We'll love her like she was our very own."

The Goolagongs agreed to let Evonne go. "Come back and see us," they said.

She promised that she would.

Evonne had to work very hard after she left peaceful Barellan. There were tennis lessons, of course. Vic Edwards had a large and famous tennis school. He had trained many champions.

But Edwards also wanted Evonne to get a good education and to be at ease in public. She took speaking lessons and went to business school.

Even though she was still timid, she began to delight people with her good manners. Some athletes are tense and rude. But not Evonne. She kept smiling even when it was hard to do.

Sometimes she was homesick for her family. She went home for visits, but never thought about giving up tennis. It was too exciting. She could not imagine anything but a tennis career.

People flocked to watch her play. At first she was afraid that they were only interested in her because she was an Aboriginal. This bothered her. "I want them to like me because I'm a good player," she said, "not because I'm part-black."

She won more than 80 tournaments by the time she was 18, in 1970.

"Now you are ready for Wimbledon," Vic Edwards said.

On a visit home to Barellan, Evonne hopped on a motorcycle and helped round up some sheep for fun. The job used to be done on horseback, but now bikes make the whole thing easier. The sheep dog sitting on the back is alert for woolly stragglers.

Although she lost at Wimbledon in 1970, Evonne did win the British Hard Court championship, 6-2, 6-0.

But she wasn't really. America's Peaches Bartkowicz knocked her out in the second round. Wimbledon, the top tennis contest in the world, was won by Margaret Smith Court.

Mrs. Court, also an Australian, was Evonne's tennis idol. She had won Wimbledon twice before—in 1965 and 1963. Now she was talking about retiring. How Evonne longed to take her place!

In 1970, Evonne entered 21 other European tournaments. She won seven of them. Now she was known all over the world. Many reporters pestered her with questions about her race.

Evonne tried to be polite. But finally she got tired of it. "Go away," she said, "or I'll point the bone at you!"

When an Aboriginal tribe does that to somebody, the person dies!

17

In 1970, Margaret Smith Court won the women's Grand Slam of tennis—Wimbledon, Forest Hills, and the French and Australian championships.

On February 1, 1971, Mrs. Court met Evonne Goolagong for the Victoria State Championship in Melbourne, Australia. It was a contest Court had won seven times.

But this time she lost—to 19-year old Evonne. The victories weren't easy. Evonne whipped Court 7-6, 7-6, with both sets decided by tie-breakers. However, even the champion herself said later that Evonne clearly out-played her. It was an exciting tennis upset.

A few weeks later, Evonne played against Court again for the Australian championship. Only a cramp in Evonne's leg prevented her from defeating the older woman again.

Some people began to wonder whether Vic Edwards had been wrong about predicting a 1974 top championship for Evonne. Maybe she was ready now!

Mrs. Court said: "I will retire at the end of 1971. Meanwhile, I want to help Evonne all I can and play as much as possible with her."

Evonne was very happy and proud.

Margaret Smith Court seems to be sizing up her young rival in this picture, taken before a game in 1971.

She also remained very unspoiled. Fame did not impress her very much. Unlike many woman players, she was not ruthless. She felt sorry when she beat an opponent. Vic Edwards worried a little about her lack of "killer instinct."

A more serious flaw in her game showed up. She seemed not to take some matches seriously enough. She would lose concentration.

She called this "going walkabout." It referred to a trait of the Aboriginal workers. If white people pushed them too hard, they would simply vanish into the wilderness.

Evonne had to retreat into her own mind.

She won both the New Zealand and the French championships. She also went with Margaret Court to play in South Africa. There she was beaten in the finals by Mrs. Court.

She may have had other things on her mind.

South Africa was a country with strict race segregation, by law. It refused to allow Arthur Ashe, a black American player, to even enter the country. But South Africa had labeled Evonne an "honorary white" and let her compete.

Other Aboriginals criticized Evonne for playing in a racist country. But she said: "I don't think I'm doing anything wrong. And besides, Mr. Edwards wants me to go."

As always, she would do what her beloved coach and foster father wanted.

Evonne holds a bouquet of flowers and the trophy symbolizing the French Women's Singles Title, which she won in 1971.

Smiling and confident, Evonne goes after one of Margaret Court's serves during the 1971 Wimbledon matches.

Evonne was seeded third at Wimbledon in 1971. The British crowds were charmed by her and made her their favorite.

"Just keep your mind on the game," said Edwards. "Don't go walkabout!"

Evonne played against Lesley Hunt. She lost the first set, 1-6. "What did I tell you?" asked her coach sternly. She smiled and said she'd do better. Then she went out and beat Hunt in the next two sets, 6-2, 6-1.

In the quarter-finals, she defeated Nancy Richey Gunter 6-3, 6-2. Then it was time to play Billie Jean King.

22

Billie Jean was a perfect example of a woman player with a killer instinct. She rushed the net like a man and had won Wimbledon's women's singles title in 1966, 1967, and 1968. She was the top money-winner among women players. Even though the British crowd did not like her, many felt she was a better player than Margaret Court—and far ahead of sweet little Evonne Goolagong.

To the surprise of everyone, King the superwoman played a mediocre game. The meek little Aboriginal destroyed Billie Jean, 6-4, 6-4.

But there were still the finals, and defending champion Margaret Court.

Evonne upset Mrs. Court in only 63 minutes to win at Wimbledon. Here she shows the fluid movement that makes winning seem so easy.

Court was a power player with blistering services. Like Billie Jean King, she would charge the net. But in many ways, she was more careful than Evonne. She would block vicious serves back into play and go for winning shots later.

Evonne was different. Her most lethal shot was a classic bankhand drive. She had a typical woman's baseline game—no razzle-dazzle rushing for her. When she kept her mind on the game, she could cover the court like a gazelle, hardly ever allowing the ball to escape her.

When a tough shot came her way, Evonne would whack away at it, trying to win points. She was willing to take chances. Was it because she was so young and strong?

At Centre Court, Wimbledon, 1971, Evonne Goolagong was a marvel of grace and power. She seemed to be skipping over the court, smiling, as Mrs. Court sent her most powerful shots over the net. Evonne responded with deadly effect.

She crushed the former champion, 6-4, 6-1.

Britain's Princess Alexandra presented Evonne with the trophy that was the highest award of the entire women's tennis world.

Later that year, she was voted top woman athlete by the Associated Press and honored as a Member of the British Empire by Queen Elizabeth.

And—perhaps the best award of all—she was named Australian of the Year.

Evonne holds high the Wimbledon trophy.

Evonne and Chris Evert shake hands after their 1972 semi-final match at Wimbledon.

In 1972, there was new excitement in women's tennis. Another young star, American Chris Evert, had risen. Everyone waited eagerly for a match between her and Evonne.

Both girls were superb players. But they had very different styles. Evonne was loose and full of imagination. Chris had a stiff, businesslike way of playing the game.

At Wimbledon that year, Evonne had to fight hard to defeat Russia's Olga Morozova in the quarter-finals. Then she met Chris in the semis. It was a tennis battle to remember.

British papers and British tennis fans were pulling for Evonne to lick Billie Jean King at Wimbledon in 1972.

Chris unloaded her baseline artillery. She won the first set, 6-4. Then she racked up a 3-0 lead in the second set.

Evonne began to pick away at the blonde American. Her strategy was to hit short to Chris's two-handed backhand and close into the net. She won the second set, 6-3.

In the third set, Evonne and Chris fought an evenly matched contest to 4-4. Evonne held serve and then broke Chris to take the set, 6-4, and the match.

Going full stretch, Evonne makes a high forehand volley against Billie Jean King in the 1972 finals at Wimbledon.

The final match, played against Billie Jean King, was an anti-climax. The crowd clearly was on the side of Evonne. Everyone hoped she would defend her title successfully against the tough, competitive Billie Jean.

But Evonne lost the first set, 6-3. In the second set, she tried to come from behind and was able to run down most of Billie Jean's attempts at a match point. But then King gave up her backhand game and sent a short, topspin shot bombing crosscourt. It was a winner. Groans were heard from the crowd as Billie Jean King tossed her racquet into the air in victory.

But later, as Mrs. King held aloft her trophy, no one clapped harder than Evonne Goolagong.

Billie Jean smiles widely as she holds her victory bouquet. But the loudest applause went to the loser, Evonne Goolagong.

A writer said of Evonne:

"Nature gave her the gifts to become a champion. But her will does not insist that she should exploit them all the time."

Some great players, such as Billie Jean King, thought it was a shame that Evonne didn't go all out, all the time. Later in 1972, Evonne lost the Bonne Bell Cup and the National Clay Court to Chris Evert. Both times, she "went walkabout," losing her concentration.

But it didn't seem to bother Evonne. Why did others take it so seriously? Evonne never felt that "winning was the only thing."

Evonne and Chris Evert meet before a match in Cleveland in 1972.

In 1973, Margaret Smith Court was back, after retiring briefly to have a baby. She and Evonne were very good friends—but that did not stop Mrs. Court from beating Evonne in the finals of the Australian Open.

Evonne led the Australian team to victory in the Federation Cup matches (women's equivalent to the Davis Cup). She reached the semi-finals of the French championship, only to lose to Margaret Court again. Then, in Italy, she whipped Chris Evert soundly, 6-0 in the second set, to win that title for the first time.

Evonne battles Margaret Court in the 1973 Australian Open.

The year 1973 was far from over. Wimbledon was a disappointment again. Billie Jean King defeated Evonne in the semi-finals on her way to taking the crown again. But Evonne won the Canadian Open.

For the first time, she made the finals at Forest Hills in the women's singles of the U.S. Open. But the title eluded her. Margaret Court won in three sets.

In 1974, Evonne won her country's championship for the first time, defeating Chris Evert.

After several losses in a row to Chris Evert, Evonne defeated her in the Bonne Bell Cup match. By winning the Bonne Bell, Australia completed a sweep of all major team competitions over the United States in 1973.

Then came the Australian Open. For the first time, Mr. and Mrs. Goolagong came from Barellan to watch their famous daughter play. In spite of blistered feet, Evonne gave Chris Evert a tough fight and won her country's tennis title for the first time.

Evonne Goolagong of the Pittsburgh Triangles playing in a World Team Tennis match in 1974.

For many years, even the best women tennis players made far less money than men. Evonne made a comfortable living from tennis. She was able to buy her parents' house and give it to them as a present. But she was far from rich.

Militant women such as Billie Jean King finally forced a change. The prizes in women's tournaments slowly increased until they were almost as high as the men's prizes. All women players, including Evonne, benefited. They were no longer second-class tennis citizens.

When Billie Jean King beat Bobby Riggs in 1973, she did a great thing for women's tennis. She gave the game priceless publicity. People who had never cared about tennis now became interested in the game. Matches that once attracted small groups of fans now had large audiences.

Women's tennis teams prospered. The best players signed with them. In 1974, Evonne Goolagong signed with the Pittsburgh Triangles. Now, besides playing in major tournaments, she would play in the World Team Tennis games.

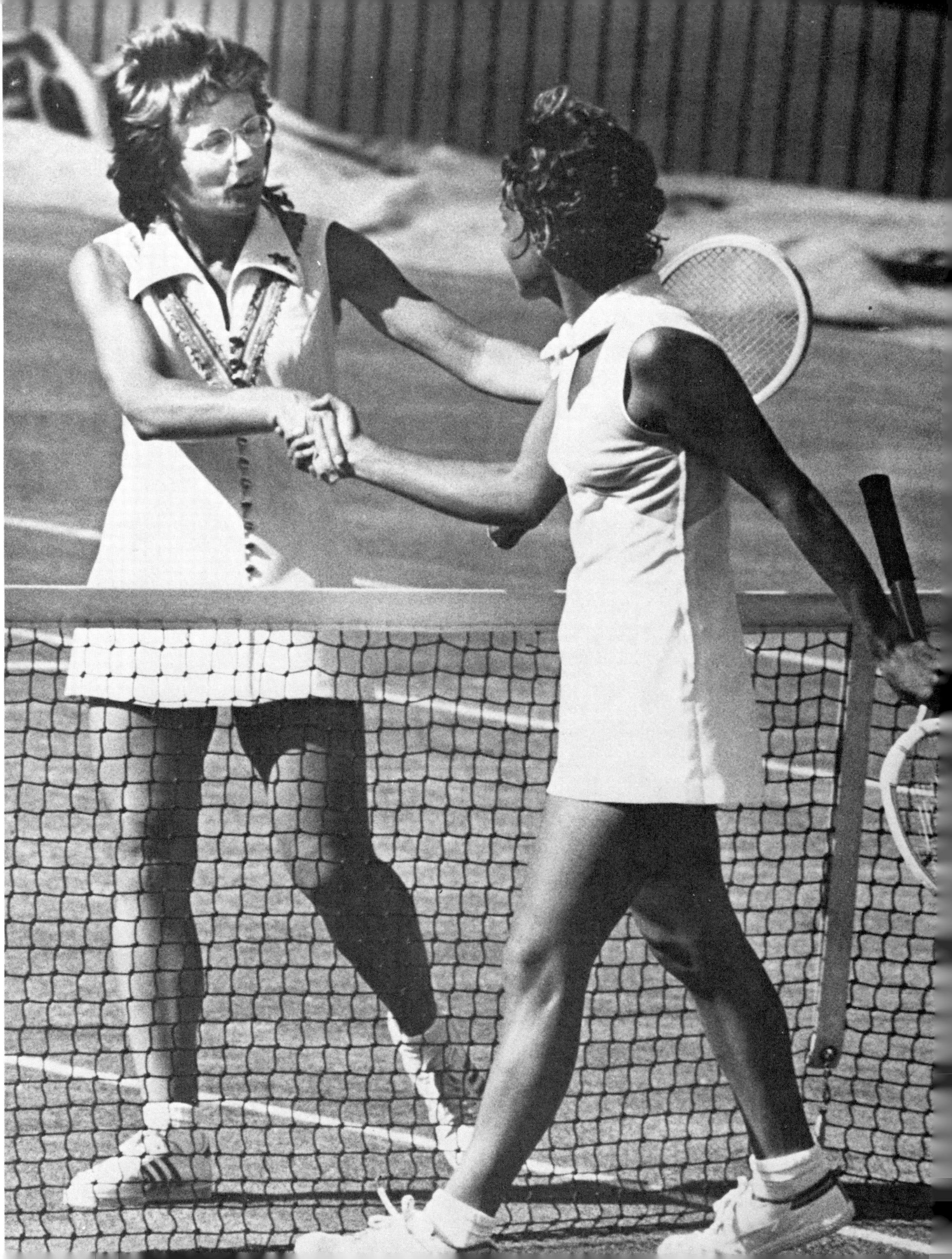

Evonne's favorite recreations include golf. Here she limbers up with a putter before starting a tour of the links.

After a brief rest at home, Evonne went to the United States. There she joined the Virginia Slims tour of the women's pro tennis circuit.

She was able to beat Billie Jean King in several matches. Most tennis fans felt that Mrs. King was now over the hill. They looked to Evonne and to Chris Evert for the future.

37

Evonne had come a long way from remote Barellan. She was no longer shy, but she had kept the sunny nature that endeared her to the fans and to other players as well.

At the age of 22, she was bright and sociable. She liked to go dancing and to pop concerts. She liked clothes and she liked boys.

"But I'm not ready to marry yet," she said. "When I do, I would rather that my husband had nothing to do with tennis!"

In Evonne's home town of Barellan, snow never falls. She first saw the cold, white stuff at Akron, Ohio and decided to sample it.

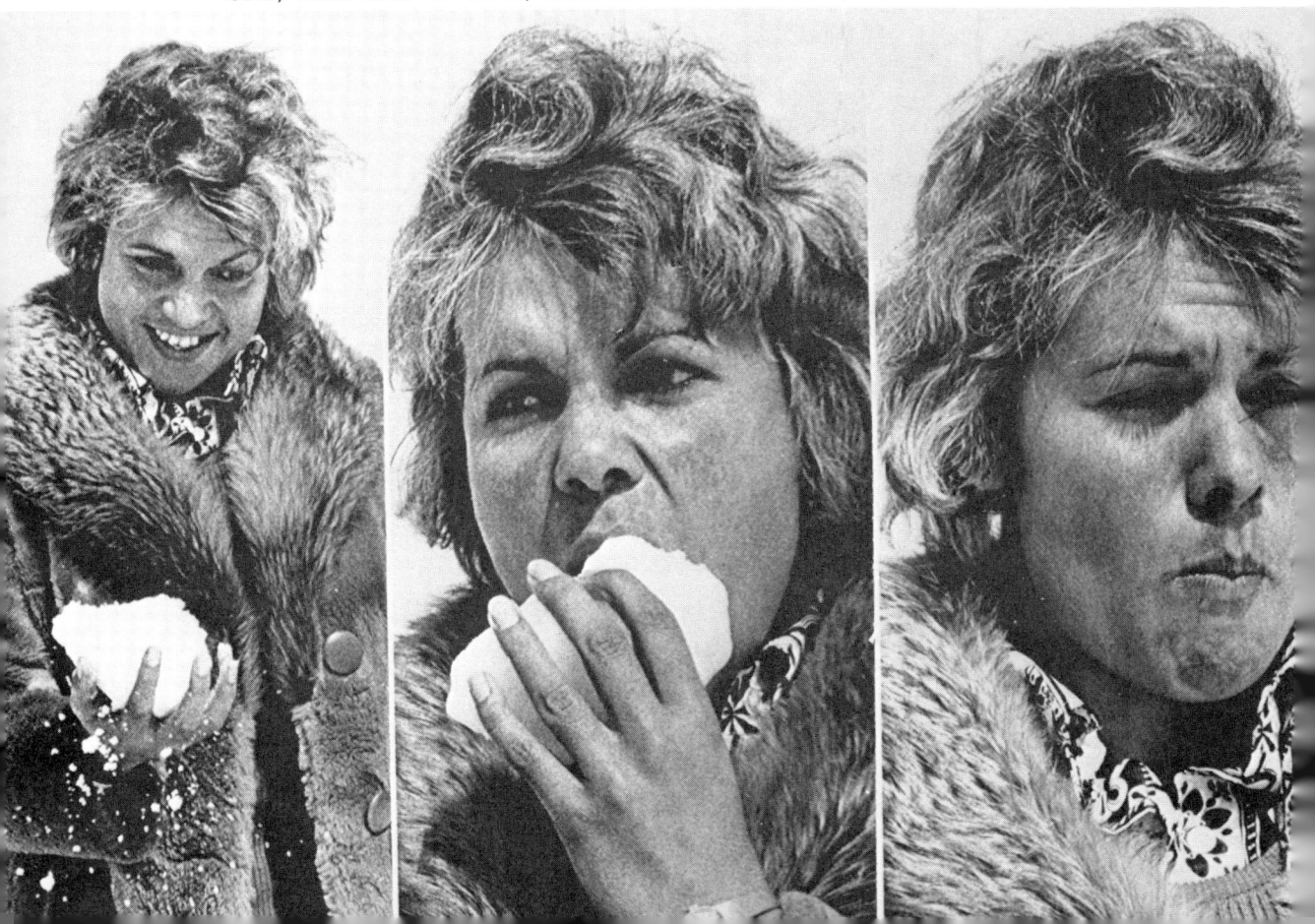

Other Aboriginals still pressed her to become a Black Power spokeswoman in Australia. But she did not want to become a militant. The role didn't fit her. She was not angry enough and she felt uncomfortable around those who were.

So her fight for the "Aboriginal cause" was a quiet kind of war. She said: "I must do my part by doing the thing I am best at—playing tennis."

The 1974 Wimbledon saw Evonne seeded third. But she lost in the quarters and saw Chris Evert put away Olga Morozova for the British title.

At Forest Hills in 1974, Evonne knocked off Kerry Melville in the quarter-finals.

Then she faced Chris Evert in the semis. A huge TV audience watched this match. Miss Evert was riding a 52-game winning streak. It seemed that no one would stop her.

Evonne won the first set 6-0, playing at the top of her form. She led 4-3 in the second set when the match was halted by rain and not resumed until two days later.

The man who is almost single-handedly responsible for tennis fashions is tall Teddy Tinling, posing here with some of his favorite clients. From left to right the women are: Virginia Wade, Evonne Goolagong, Rosie Casals, and Billie Jean King. Before Tinling began to design, women's tennis clothes were plain white dresses.

The second set was forced into a tie breaker. Despite having several match points against her, Chris rallied to win, 7-6.

First-seeded Evert and fifth-seeded Goolagong now entered the exciting finale of their match. They were playing on grass—not Evert's best surface. Evonne flitted about easily and reached match point four times. Chris held her off—then fell at last, 6-3. Her winning streak had been snapped.

Billie Jean King defends her title at the 1974 U.S. Open at Forest Hills.

Evonne misses one of Billie Jean's shots at Forest Hills.

In the finals against Billie Jean King, Evonne had to fight very hard. Mrs. King was eager to show that there was life in the old girl yet. She was magnificent in the first set. But the Aboriginal girl was flawless!

Evonne took the first set, 6-3.

Striking back, Mrs. King won the second set, 6-3.

Evonne forged ahead in the third set, 3-0. She broke Billie Jean's serve. But unfortunately she could not hold her own. Mrs. King rallied and finally took the set, 7-5.

Evonne had lost, but it had been one of her most exciting games.

Two weeks later, Evonne repeated her victory over Chris Evert with a win in the finals at Denver. The two girls now stood 7-7 in major championships. Their rivalry was more exciting to fans than the exploits of the best male players—or even the awesome victories of Billie Jean King.

The last important tennis event of 1974 was the Virginia Slims championship. It was a contest worth $100,000 to the players. The winner would receive $32,000, the richest prize ever awarded to a woman in tennis.

Before the semi-final match, Billie Jean King confessed to reporters that she was nervous. "I was nervous before I played Evonne in Forest Hills, too. She is very, very good."

Unlike King, Evonne was loose and relaxed for the tournament. "I have nothing to lose!" she said cheerfully. And she proceeded to beat everyone.

She beat Billie Jean King in the semis. Then she met Chris Evert for the finals. Rushing the net to perfection, she offered a series of tough shots to Evert. Some people wondered where her old baseline game had gone!

Evert was rarely able to smash or lob the ball past Evonne. And at the end, the Australian girl was the winner, 6-3, 6-4.

Evonne is presented with the Virginia Slims trophy by Jim Morgan of the Philip Morris Company, which sponsors the tournament.

Vic Edwards leads Evonne through an airport during her annual tennis tour. When she is not playing, Evonne lives with Mr. and Mrs. Edwards at their home near Sydney, Australia.

She was still far, far from being a "killer." Her new game was more aggressive. But why shouldn't she change? She was growing. So should her game. Her faithful coach, Vic Edwards, was still there to guide her. But she alone had to decide the best way to play.

She was a champion, but a very young one. And the best was yet to come. Whatever challenges waited for her, Evonne Goolagong was ready to meet them with a smile.